My Senses

Leon Read

SEA-TO-SEA

Mankato Collingwood London

Contents

Look for Tiger on the pages of this book. Sometimes he is hiding.

We have five senses.

hearing

seeing

tasting

touching

smelling

Seeing

We see things with our eyes.

What are you using your eyes for now?

Billy wears glasses.

His sight is blurry without them.

When it's dark

It is hard to see in the dark.

I like the dark.
I play with
my flashlight.

We need light to see.

What other things light up the dark?

Hearing

We hear sounds
with our ears.

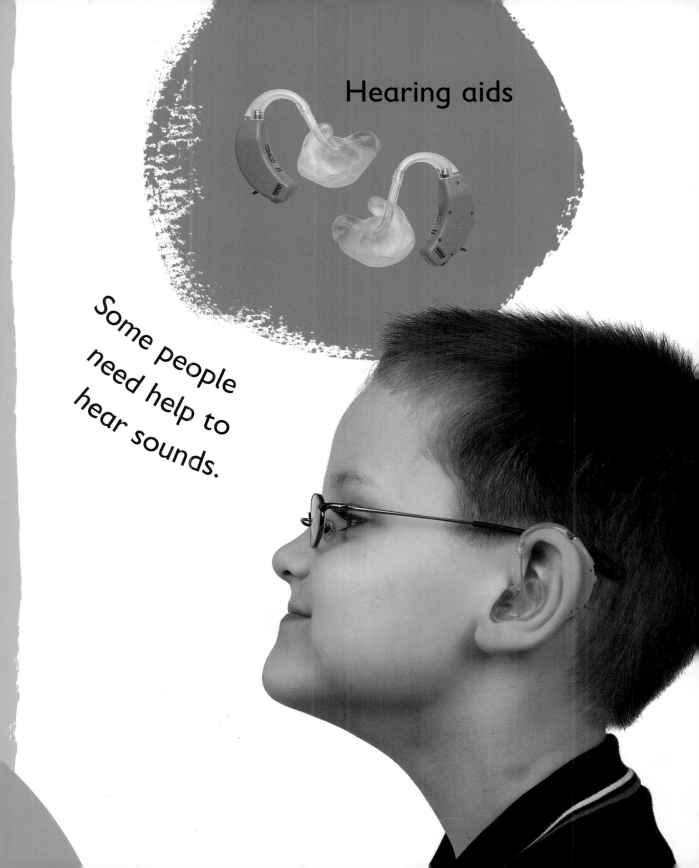

Hearing aids

Some people need help to hear sounds.

Sounds around

We hear sounds almost all the time.

tweet tweet

I recorded some of my favorite sounds.

Touching

We touch with our skin.
Our fingers are good
at feeling things.

When I touch
water, it
feels wet.

Billy and Grace
like Tiger.
He feels soft.

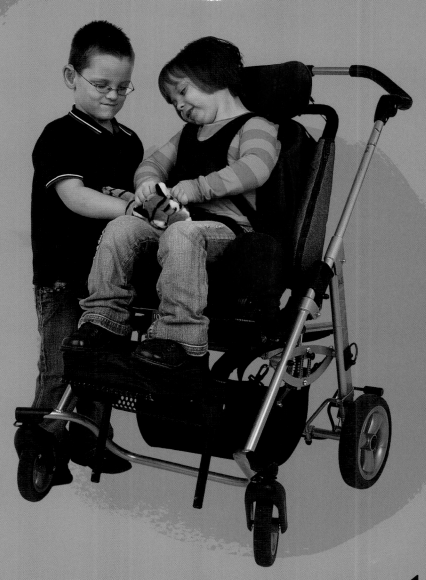

13

Smelling

We smell things
with our nose.

Some things smell nice.

foamy soap

Some things smell bad.

stinky sock

Smell and tell

Smelling things helps us tell what they are. You can play a fruit-smelling game.

I mixed up the boxes. Then I guessed which fruit was in each box.

Tasting

We taste food and drink
with our tongue.

This is a list of all my favorite flavors.

What are your favorite flavors?

Staying safe

Our senses help us to stay safe.

How do our senses help us stay safe on a busy street?

How do our senses tell us when food is not safe to eat?

I took a picture of some stinky, moldy cheese.

Super senses

tasting

smelling

seeing

We have
five senses.

hearing

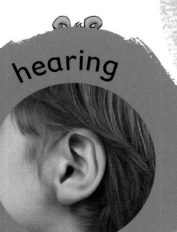

touching

Alex is making a
senses collage.

Find pictures
in old
magazines
and make a
collage of
your own.

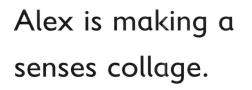

Word picture bank

Glasses—P. 5

Hearing aid—P. 9

Light—P. 7

Moldy—P. 21

Stinky—P. 15

Wet—P. 12

This edition first published in 2010 by Sea-to-Sea Publications
Distributed by Black Rabbit Books
P.O. Box 3263, Mankato, Minnesota 56002
Copyright © Sea-to-Sea Publications 2010

Printed in USA

9 8 7 6 5 4 3 2

Published by arrangement with the Watts Publishing Group Ltd,
London.

Library of Congress Cataloging-in-Publication Data
Read, Leon.
  My senses / Leon Read.
     p. cm. -- (Tiger talk. All about me)
  Includes index.
  ISBN 978-1-59771-188-3 (hardcover)
  1. Senses and sensation--Juvenile literature. I. Title.
  QP434.R43 2010

612.8--dc22

                    2008045010

Series editor: Adrian Cole
Photographer: Andy Crawford

Design: Sphere Design Associates
Art director: Jonathan Hair
Consultants: Prue Goodwin and Karina Law

Acknowledgments:
The Publisher would like to thank Norrie Carr model agency
and Scope. "Tiger" puppet used with kind permission from
Ravensden PLC (www.ravensden.co.uk).
Tiger Talk logo drawn by
Kevin Hopgood.

There are 18 Tigers, including me, in this book.
Did you find all of us?